INTENTIONAL

TRANSFORMATION

Intentional Transformation is a practical text, an easy read, that will provide you, the reader with a spiritually moving experience. My text will challenge you to delve into the depths of your inner most being, ask yourself critical questions, renounce every excuse, every hindrance and justifiable action, all for the purpose of getting the rest of God's Best for your life. It is for those who are willing to seek the undiscovered you. My friend, Simon Bailey, author of the best seller, Release Your Brilliance, challenges us to find our brilliance that we were born with. Intentional Transformation screams, find it and then the scream gets louder, find it now! **Intentional Transformation** demands that you be the self-acting agent in this process and that you give no resistance to the work of the Holy Spirit who will participate and partner with you to finish this work. **Intentional Transformation** is so powerful. It doesn't wait until the end to yield change, it starts as soon as you start.

Judy Shaw Foundation
1115 South Holly Drive
Sioux Falls, SD 57105

INTENTIONAL

TRANSFORMATION

HOW TO INTENTIONALLY EXPERIENCE
THE TRANSFORMATIONAL POWER OF GOD

JUDY SHAW

Judy Shaw Foundation

"You are holding in your hand a key to your next dimension. Judy comes alongside us as a transformational whisperer who prods, nudges, and pulls us out of our comfort zones. Her rawness is refreshing in a world of political correctness. Every person you know needs a copy of "Intentional Transformation". This will save them thousands of dollars sitting on the sofa for counseling and give them the kick start to live by choice instead of by circumstance. Thank you Judy for allowing us to see into the window of your soul. Our spirits are uplifted and challenged to live with fearless intention as we transform from the inside out. Bravo!"

Simon T. Bailey
Author of the best selling book "Release Your Brilliance"
Creator of the Shift Your Brilliance System

"I am honored to be asked to write an endorsement for Judy Shaw. Judy is one of the most "real" people I have ever met. Her is what I respect about her—she comes from her heart! Her caring is not a show; it is the REAL DEAL! Her love for people is constantly expressed in the work she has and is doing with helping others improve their life. I connected with her the first time I met her, because what she is doing with her life is her "ministry." She is living her God Calling! Many don't understand ministry, but simply speaking it is dedicating your life to help others learn the Love God has for all people. Learning from those who are living their "God Calling" are the people you want to help guide your life. Judy Shaw is one of those people!"

Richard Flint
Speaker, Author and Founder of Richard Flint Intl.

"I along with countless others, have benefited immensely from Judy. Godly wisdom discernment and a refusal to give up on her Mission as a Kingdom Builder. I always admire her love and passion to the lost souls. Keep touching lives for you've touched mine!"

Kathy Roberson Bowman
Author of "Steps to Living in God's Light"
Director and Founder of Kathy Bowman Ministries

"Judy has a gift I have not seen in any other speaker. When she speaks she inspires love, joy and hope with every word; she has the rare ability to touch people in all walks of life."

Allen Madison
Allen Madison Associate Professor of Law, J.D., LL.M.
University of South Dakota

"I've had the distinct pleasure of knowing Judy for over 25 years. When I think of her the words bold and innovative come to mind. She's a critical thinker with insight beyond her years. Her revelatory understanding of the times and seasons has shaped her to manifest what her father could only dream about."

Bishop Joseph A. McCargo
Sr Pastor and Founder City of Hope International Worship Centre
President, United Kingdom Network of Churches, Ministries and Businesses

"The love of Jesus permeates everything Judy Shaw does. She is passionate in her ministry to the hurting of this world whether it's rescuing enslaved women in a foreign country or helping a patient overcome addiction at Keystone in South Dakota. Her book will be a blessing to many."

Carol Regier
CEO, Keystone Treatment Center, Canton South Dakota

"Judy Shaw, the real Relationship Pastor, true and dependable friend whose story can be written until the end of the world. Judy is one of the Spiritual Leaders of our time that come only once. From her testimony of how God saved her life in a terrible accident to the work that she has dedicated her life to do, Judy in her faithfulness to God and His mission, demonstrates a vibrant and compelling relationship with God in Christ; responds to the power of the Holy Spirit in daily life and is amazingly obedient to Christ's mission to go and make disciples. Her resilience easily handles disappointment while maintaining effectiveness."

Hon Rev Kenn Nyagudi
Former Member of the National Assembly of Kenya
International Director & Preacher, Knowledge International Ministries

"Pastor Judy Shaw is the most powerful communicator of God's word I have ever met. This is because God has been leading her every step of the way and she has been willing to blindly follow. She has a life story that will bring you to tears and restore your faith. No matter how far down you have gone this story will lift you up."

Dr. Ron Perkinson
Clinical Director of Keystone Treatment
Center, Canton, S.D.
Author of "Chemical Dependency Counseling"
(Leading treatment manual in the world for Chemical dependency counselors)

"As I have traveled abroad with Pastor Judy numerous times, I witnessed her unconditional love and dedication to the call of God on her life. Her humility and genuineness changed my life forever. My entire family as well enjoyed being a part of God's healing transformational work in the lives of the Maasai people."

Dr. Mark Hagen Sr.
Chiropractic Specialist in Sioux Falls, S.D.

"Blessings in life come from God. There is great favor over the life of Judy Shaw. She carries the keys of wisdom and knowledge because of years of dedication and devotion to God. She chooses wisely and precisely. Judy carries with her a never ending provision purse of love and passion for people wherever she goes. She is a giver of life's greatest treasure—friendship, family, and love. Now, from the purse of her heart that carries her most personal possessions comes her book. 'Intentional Transformation.'"

Dan and Gina Blaze
Directors of The New England Prayer Center

*"The world has been waiting for the release of this amazing Woman of God's step by step revelation of her **Intentional Transformation** journey. Exceptionally gifted by God, Pastor Judy's life and ministry, have engaged, inspired and transformed the lives of tens of thousands around the world, including my own. Her continued obedience to the will of God, has catapulted Pastor Judy into this Kairos moment, where her transparency and intentional obedience have collided with the pages of this inspiring account of the purposeful, miraculous transformation of her life. May your life be forever changed. A **"must read"**!"*

Althea Sims
Co-Pastor, The Dwelling Place COGIC; 2nd Vice President, International Sunday School Department, Church of God in Christ, Inc.

"Lots of christian leaders today talk about creativity and experience in ministries. Judy Shaw truly defines it in practice not just in theory. Her life, friendship, and prophetic vision, bring reality of God strategy, show you how to make breakthroughs and set your spiritual bar high—and keep it there. As church planter, pastor, and apostolic influencer in the Balkan area and Middle East, I found honest, purpose driven, apostolic support in Judy Shaw that help the church planting movement to grow, mature, and manifest God's image in this area of the world."

Radovan Bogdanovic
Church Planter and Leader of Kingsway Connection Movement in Serbia, Macedonia, Greece, Turkey, and Middle East

"Inimitable is the word that describes Judy Shaw. Her very life spells the word "intentional". She's a truth seeker and releaser. As you read her book, you will observe her unique approach and delivery to convey clarity and understanding that will inspire you to consciously measure your pursuit. This book will open your eyes and challenge you to have a crucial conversation with yourself. It is practical, insightful, powerful and most of all, purposeful. Thanks, Judy, for being an example for my life."

Pastor Paula Cook-Smith
Spiritual Advisor, Recording Artist

DEDICATION

I dedicate this book... to my "international parents" who had spiritual instinct and insight which caused them to began shaping my life at a very early age.

My Dad, Bishop Carl Roberson, my mentor, best critic, encourager, teacher and the list goes on. If he was still present in physical form, his words would probably be;

> "Judy, You are just like me, I have taught you well! Now, with what you know added with all that you have learned from me, you will go further than I could ever go".

How do I know this? He's spoken these words to me at a couple of times throughout my journey. He was always there! Dad, thanks for not quitting. Through it all, there are hundreds of sons and daughters you have influenced shouting "Thank you, Bishop, for finishing your course!"

My dear, precious Mom, who can compare to Gertie C. Roberson? Priceless. The epitome of humility, elegant, caring, one who loved to serve God by serving people, my #1 fan and one of the greatest Business women I have ever known. If Mom was yet present with us, without a doubt, she would have every published book sold all by herself! Family, am I telling the truth?

Mom, we miss you so much, you too taught us so much by precept and example!

Special acknowledgement and thanks... to The Throne Publishing Group family, thanks for your patience with me doing my first book. We did it! My "rah-rah"team staying on me, helping me to "get her done". Pam Karlen, Paula Smith-Cook, Josh Duncan, Iva Spooner, Tracey Turnquist. Stacy Nielsen thanks for your intercession.

Special thanks to Bishop Joseph and Andrea McCargo, Bishop Michael and Aimee Cole for always supporting and being covenant partners throughout my journey.

TABLE OF CONTENTS

FOREWORD

"Intentional Transformation" is a book that I have been waiting for someone to write. We all have a destiny. Everyone has a desire to pursue the destiny that God has for their life. The scripture says that God wrote our names in the book of life before the foundation of the world. That means that God wrote the story or destiny of our life before He created matter. That is a wonderful fact. However, we ask ourselves how we can become the person who has the ability to fulfill the destiny that God wrote about us. This book will tell you "how" to get to the place where you can literally become the person who is capable of fulfilling your destiny.

The more I read this manuscript the more I am convinced that this is the book I have been looking and waiting for someone to write. This book tells me how I can become the person that God can use to fulfill His purpose for my life.

This is not a book about good intentions. Many of us have good intentions but never reach our divine destiny. We all know that we can never reach God's dream for our lives unless our lives have a divine encounter with God. We envision a powerful encounter with

God that will transform us into the person that not only pursues God, but the person who finds a God who can transform them.

All of us want to be righteous, but no one is capable of being righteous. The only hope for us to be righteous is to have the righteousness of God himself placed in our spirit so we become a reflection of the divine nature. Then, and only then can the human being become the righteousness of God in Christ.

And most of us desire to pursue and find our purpose in life, but we know the person we are today can never become the fulfillment of the destiny or purpose that God has designed for us.

That is why Judy Shaw had to write "Intentional Transformation". John Wesley said, "God does nothing except in answer to Prayer". I agree. However, let me make an equally profound statement. "God can never fulfill His Purpose for your life UNLESS you become the person who is re-created in the image of Christ with an innate 'God ability' to be the person that fulfills their God destiny."

So, Judy, you did it! You created a book with the profound truth that we can never become the person that can fulfill "Divine Purpose", unless we are transformed. And we can never be transformed unless we seek God and "His Transformation."

I love Judy's words at the beginning of the book when she says that this kind of transformation require a definitive approach, mindset and strategy. She further states "that to be intentional" we must have a goal, chart a course toward the goal, calculate the cost and be wiling to pay the price to achieve our goal. We then and only then can move forward in our pursuit and have an absolute resolve to succeed. I agree, Judy, and you told me how to do that.

Or the bottom line, you tell me how to be intentional in my pursuit of transformation. I learn as I read these pages that this kind of transformation is the continual work of God in my life. And as I read through the pages, I discovered things about myself I never knew before.

I urge the reader to really be very introspective as you read the story of Judy's auto accident and the transformation that took place in her life as God not only gave her a miracle recovery, but she accepted the responsibility to invite the transforming God into her pain and suffering. She truly permitted this experience as opening the door to "Intentional. Transformation."

So, today, you have a choice. This manuscript says that every day a person has only two choices. Those two choices are that we can feed the confusion or strengthen the clarity. After you read these words, you can continue to feed the confusion in our life concerning purpose and destiny, or you can open your heart to the beauty and wonder of Judy's words and let these words erase the confusion and strengthen the clarity of vision as you pursue "Intentional Transformation."

I pray as Judy said in the last statements in this book, "My desire is that this book has inspired you to act….and act intentionally."

So be intentional. Get and read your copy of "Intentional Transformation" and read it today. It will lead you to the greatest experience of your life.

Bishop Tommy Reid

Best Selling Author, International Pastor and Evangelist

INTRODUCTION

The most important journey you will take in your life will usually be the one of self transformation. Often, this is the scariest because it requires the greatest changes in your life.

—*Shannon L. Alder*

Transformation requires an approach, mindset, and strategy. And I describe this course of action with one word: intentionality. To be intentional means:

1. You have a goal and have charted your course toward it;
2. You have calculated the cost and decided you will pay it;
3. You have studied and devised a strategy to move forward;
4. And finally, you have an absolute resolve to succeed—and abide by no excuses.

That's intentionality! However, given the state of language today, it's easy to confuse being *intentional* with merely having *good intentions.* Being intentional is all of the things I said above, and more. Good intentions, though, are little more than thoughts.

A sentiment like, "Wouldn't it be nice if things were different?" is nothing but a *good intention* until it turns to action. Because it's not until the moment we're willing to do something that we become *intentional*. And we each have the ability to be intentional. Right now, you have this incredible power in your mind.

As you read this book, I want you to be intentional in your pursuit of transformation. This will mean purposeful procuring of the only one who can bring about lasting transformation—God himself. As you read and pray, remember that if you have the ability to think a certain way, you have the ability to be this way. But it requires commitment.

Mere *good intentions* leave the door to your mind wide open because you have not fully committed. You are not truly committed to something until it's become a course of action. Being intentional, however, locks the door and throws away the key. It's a state of living that doesn't depend upon emotions, but relies upon a godly resolve. A resolve driven by purpose, principle, and priority.

One of the things this book will show you is that this kind of transformation has a pattern. And patterns predict! Results can be predicted when a pattern is followed. So you will find instructions and directions to follow. And the first step to transformation is intentional action. I promise you this will not be a chore, but a welcomed choice. You will be ready to redesign your life according to the new you God is unveiling.

I am excited for you!

Dive into this book. But just remember, everything starts with intentional action. Join me as we allow our intentional God to do incredible work in our lives. Remember with me the words of the Apostle Paul: "being confident of this, that he who began a good work in you will carry it on to completion until the day of Christ Jesus." (Philippians 1:6)

Amen—now turn the page!

PART ONE

THE NEED

1
THE BEGINNING

Transformation requires both a pattern and a place, and the Lord is always its author. As living epistles, he writes new life in us through faithful community, sustaining us through trials, and healing our brokenness.

What if I told you that there is something about yourself that you don't know, but its insight will change your life forever? God transforms us in ways we don't expect. He takes us by surprise, providing for us in wonderful ways. Transformation is the continual work on his calendar. God's designed plan and purpose for each of us is revealed when it is in season—ripe and ready for harvest. This is the mystery of transformation that I have personally experienced. There is something unknown in us that God makes known. He reveals something that has been hidden inside of us, and through it, changes our lives forever. Often, this process begins before we even realize it. As he is faithful to begin depositing [seeds of faith] into our earthen soil, his promise is to finish what he started. So, if you're reading this book, just know that God is intentional about finishing what he has started in you.

In my life, I've discovered that transformation has both a pattern and a place. But it always begins with unexpected awareness. It's like the lights flipping on in a room that you didn't know was dark. You thought you knew yourself, every piece, every fold and fabric of your heart. Then God sends someone or something to reveal to you what you didn't know you didn't know! Transformation begins with that flicker of insight, that flash of revelation exposing and bringing to light the underlying darkness.

POWER OF TRANSFORMATION

It's only intentional transformation when truth, openness, and honesty are filtered through pure motives. It's then that they've truly entered the equation. The Apostle Paul talks about Christians having a form, or pseudotype, of godliness that falls short of the real thing. He writes to Timothy that these people will act religiously but reject the power that God wants to use to transform them (2 Timothy 3:5).

There's a long list of false characteristics, attributes, and misrepresentations of Christ from both pulpit and pew. Here's a few on the list:

- False humility;
- Extreme giftedness;

- Charismatic persona;
- Cunning and manipulative nature;
- Self-exalting;
- And self-governing.

In many cases it's true to say these weren't the original intentions of such believers. But through Satan's deception and their own quest for self-glory, somewhere the tide turned. Their original Kingdom agenda was co-opted by the kingdom of man.

For decades, I've drawn the line between the kingdom of man and the Kingdom of God. What I've learned is the kingdom of man is more external. It portrays traits, behaviors, and characteristics of man's carnal nature—which we could also call the flesh. They operate under the "look like, act like" syndrome. As they have been deceived by the gods of this world, so they must deceive others to accomplish their own goals. But their fall can be so subtle and slow, not even *they* realize it at first.

One of my famous questions relating to this kind of behavior is, "Does anybody read and believe the Bible?" Without fail, the people who don't, end up spiraling into destructive patterns and outcomes. But you should know this bit of truth. As previously stated, like King Saul, most never started that way! It's the intentional luring of the deceiver!

So when we talk about transformation, we're talking about someone who's been made new. This means set free from the fleshly ways of leadership and lifestyle. Those around them can feel and see the change in their lives. Just as Jesus opened blind eyes, strengthened lame legs, and invited a dead man to step out of the grave, he also sovereignly transforms us today. For me, a greater measure of significance entered into my life when this transformation began. Without announcement or warning, God opened my eyes to see his call in my life in a fresh way, and I jumped in wholeheartedly to take hold of it.

My prayer is, as I share episodes of my life, that you will gain deeper insight into yours. Allow me to reiterate: it is our time! There is a battle raging for the hearts of men, women, and children before our very eyes—say it with me: "Lord, open my eyes that I may see."

SLAYING THE GIANTS

Discovering God's call to ministry in my life began long before I knew it was happening. Seeds were planted along my journey, growing little by little. But even after I had pastored for years, the Lord had more transformation in store for me. As recently as 2016, with 30-plus years engaged in successful full-time ministry, another harvest time came through the words of a fellow pastor and trusted friend named Jerome. Jerome is what I consider a "sharp shooter." Through his gift of discernment and sober prophetic voice, he spoke these words to me: "Shaw, the Lord showed me a vision of you." In detail, he shared that he saw a "new me." The Lord had given him a vision of who I was supposed to be, and also of what was holding me back. I saw neither the vision nor the obstacles, but I knew three things as he spoke: his words were powerfully revealing, they went straight to my core, and everything in me said *yes*! Truth hit me like a ton of bricks.

"You have a Goliath to slay," Jerome said. "You have a war to fight. Not on the outside, but on the inside. God is bringing major transformation in your life. You are going to do things in a totally different way. The Lord is giving you fresh oil to bring healing and change to people. It won't spring from your victories, but will pour from your past experiences of pain. They see you in your glory, but they don't know your story; and Shaw, it's time to tell your story. They have no clue of what you've suffered and been through to become who you are today. In fact, not even I know the whole truth. But you can only have it if you address things in your life that you never have before. You didn't think it was important to tell so you just kept moving, surviving every hit. But now, the time has come for you to slay these giants that you have had with you for so long."

I could not deny his words. Instantly, I remembered the silent tears only I had seen and felt; tears I was determined not to let fall again. Over the years, I've had many people attempt to abort my life's calling. I've dodged many darts and bullets, and endured backstabbing. All because I ran hard to fulfill God's calling in my life. So, I simply ignored the opposition, never responded to it, and kept my gaze locked straight ahead.

In fact, I considered my non-responsiveness to be virtuous and victorious, especially because I was on a mission and couldn't bear the thought of slowing down. After all, I had things to do, places to go, and people to see.

However, I remember well an afternoon conversation with one of my staff, Pastor Iva. With a hand on her hip, she said, "Pastor, why are you still trying to help these people? You know they just stabbed you in your back for no reason at all."

I replied, "Well, what do you want me to do? I'm the pastor—I can't stab them back!"

We had a good laugh at that before leaving the office. Even now, I don't share any of this to garner sympathy or host a pity party. My sole desire has been to keep charging ahead, not looking to the right or the left. The reward I covet is hearing the Lord say, "Well done, faithful daughter."

However, I must confess, I did often wonder why no one saw my deep pain or sensed my hurting heart. I thought, "I can sense others' needs; can't they sense mine?" I learned to take my solace and encouragement in being a spiritual warrior, understanding it simply comes with the territory. If you're in this place, take heart that the Lord sees you, too—*just as he always saw me.* We must keep running toward the crown.

Jerome's words brought King David to mind, the boy who killed Goliath with a sling and a stone. Also, I thought of Samuel and what God told him: "Do not look on his appearance… For the LORD *sees* not as man sees: man looks on the outward appearance, but the LORD looks on the heart." (1 Sam 16:7) The Lord sees our hearts, and that is the first place he works. God gave my friend those words of knowledge for me. He had insight into my heart and future that I didn't even have. But this is often how God's transformation in us begins. It begins with revealing what has been concealed—unearthing things of the heart that were buried, forgotten, and even unknown. But the Lord often speaks truth through godly people in our lives. And when he does, we have to *listen*. Everybody needs a Jerome in their life.

Jerome continued, explaining the giants that were lined up on the battlefield of my life. He said, "You have slain lions and won battles. But you still have to deal with yourself; with why you've allowed so much injustice against yourself. People see you as strong and put together, but now you have to address the low self-esteem and shame they never see you struggling with."

When we avoid dealing with pain hidden in our lives, we also avoid growth and forfeit the transformation God has for us. At Keystone Treatment Center, our beds are filled with clients who have found ways to numb, medicate, and deny their deep-seated pain and dysfunction. And all this does is delay the inevitable. However, at the point of this epiphany, I wanted every area of my life to pass the scrutiny of this truth, too. I needed to know what else I was blind to and unaware of. I was not interested in prolonging my ignorance and therefore delaying my spiritual growth. I had to dive deeper to get what I needed. Simply put, I needed to get intentional, which requires absolute resolve. Intentionality has no room for incomplete or imprecise thoughts. And this propels you to accomplishment without excuse or apologies. Intentional!

I acknowledged that I had low self-esteem. But it wasn't that bad, I thought. This sent my mind racing. Growing up, I had always pushed my sister Kathy forward, putting her in the spotlight. I even encouraged her to pursue her acting and modeling careers. To me, she was the performer and I was the introvert. She was slim and trim, I was pleasingly plump and chunky. My character was shy, quiet, and reserved. There was no jealousy; to me, it was simply who we were. She was the lead singer in the group, and I was the backup.

Instead of being the main attraction, I was the wise and humble one, content with being tucked away behind the scenes. I hid behind a curtain that I had named "virtue." Humility is honorable, but my self-view was not actually one of humility. It was one of pride and shame. And this is what the Lord was calling out in me through my trusted friend: *the pride I never even knew was there.* So there I stood, exposed by undeniable truth. Even if my mind didn't know it and couldn't perceive it, my spirit knew it very well.

This is a pattern the Lord revealed. My pride had masqueraded as humility and shame, letting me view myself as modest and reserved. I believed I was a model and example of what a godly woman should be. I had spiritualized my station in life by labeling it virtuous. After all, God resists the proud but gives grace to the humble, right? But in reality, these were covered up deep-seated insecurities and poor self-esteem. I was so fearful of what others thought of me that I stayed in what my sister called my "bubble." But as the Lord revealed these things to me, he also gave Jerome a needle to burst that bubble!

This secret pride affected other areas of my life as well. When you're afraid to look bad in front of others or disappoint them, there is a word you never say. Can you guess what it is? It's "No." When you want to make everyone else happy all of the time, especially at your own expense, you must always say yes. But it's not right. Because in the end, it depletes you. This is what pride does. It destroys while staying hidden.

To live out my calling, I had to slay the giant of pride in my life. But it wasn't the stereotypical, on-the-surface egotistical pride. Instead, it masked itself beneath the guise of protecting myself and my image of helping others. No more could I be scared or nervous to disappoint someone by saying no. No longer could I worry that my intentions or motivations would be misinterpreted. Through my transformation, it was revealed to me that what I thought was humility was actually pride. When you are willing to let truth have her perfect work—this is the moment transformation begins. I've always said, "You never stay where you start." It's a mark of maturity when you leave the immature things and begin to live in the real world.

HUNGER FOR GROWTH

Have you thought about your life? What patterns have you noticed? What's your story? What lies have you believed? Maybe you have been successful for years, but never imagined something greater would transpire if you shared both your pain and glory.

What excuses have become your walls? Perhaps the most important question of this book is related to the one Jesus asked the man at the pool of Bethesda in John 5. In my mind, I hear his question like this: "What is it that you really, seriously want? How much longer do you want to be in this condition?"

Now, do you sense a question coming your way? I think it's time to have a conversation with Jesus—and a critical one at that.

When we desire the destiny God has for us, we take the first step on a journey to a radically changed life. We become people with hearts that pant for streams of living water. We are moved to action. There is a discernable difference between who we were and who we have become. Your excitement and freedom become undeniable. What if you are void of this hunger for growth and change, and instead feel fear or inadequacy? Ask yourself, "How bad do I want it, and am I ready to pay the price to have it?" If so, begin to honestly confess what you don't have and run after it until you get it.

I remember when my father, my blessed daddy, Bishop Carl Roberson, confirmed my calling. He told me I was to be in ministry. I didn't like the idea of speaking to the multitudes—I preferred one-on-one conversations and quiet interactions. I never envisioned as myself a minister of God's word. So when my father pushed me toward Houghton Bible School to prepare myself for ministry, I thought, "That's not for me." However, after a time of prayer, I knew I had to embrace his words. That's when I fell to my knees and pleaded with God. I prayed, "God, I am not bold. If you want me to walk into full-time ministry and speak to the masses, you have to give me confidence and boldness."

I was not bold, I was timid. I was not a speaker, I was a listener. I was not the lead singer, I was the backup. But there I was, on my knees, realizing that my confidence was dead. I needed new confidence to carry out God's call. So I asked for it. Then I remembered Moses. He prayed a similar prayer, too. This is part of the pattern of God's work in his people. He reveals something that was concealed and makes provision in ways we never thought possible.

TRANSFORMED IN COMMUNITY

Just as Moses had Aaron, I had mentors, colleagues, family, and my covenant friends. They were both necessary and intentionally positioned in my life. This is why godly transformation has both a pattern and a *place*. It is a place among intentional people who also seek to do God's work. Esther needed Mordecai to open her eyes to see that she was chosen for "such a time as this..." She was the one appointed to save a nation, but she needed Mordecai's prompting. I can relate to Esther's feelings, though on a smaller scale. I never thought that I would travel the world speaking, giving hope and healing to many nations. I did not know that destiny was working behind the scenes.

Do you remember Rafiki from *The Lion King*? He was the baboon who helped Simba remember who he was when he was stuck in a rut of despair. He reminded him, "You are Mufasa's son!" Simba was reminded of his destiny and legacy. We need reminding as well, both of *who* we are and *why* we are. What I've learned is that lasting transformation only happens within a life-giving community. You need trusted voices, caring hearts, and support groups to help you finish your journey.

BROKEN PROVOCATIONS

In addition to insight from godly community, transformation also entails a breaking. Sometimes we are physically broken, other times mentally, spiritually, or even financially. But here is the truth: you cannot fix what you cannot see. When we break, that which needs to be changed inside of us is revealed. A spotlight shines on the places God is going to work on next. Trials are often the vehicle for this. They can be blessings, provocations to advancement, or growth. We can only become whole when our brokenness is exposed and mended.

Remember Joseph? There was a boy with some cockiness. He couldn't stop talking about his dreams, and his brothers didn't like the thought of bowing down to serve him very much, did they? Not at all. As the story goes, they threw him in a pit and sold him to slavers. Now, at the bottom of this pit, do you think Joseph was having some internal dialogues? I imagine him asking himself questions like, "How did I end up here? Weren't my brothers supposed to be serving me?" But his story doesn't end in the pit.

Joseph is taken to Egypt, where he is slandered, falsely accused, jailed, and forgotten. He is broken by trial after trial. Finally, despite the injustice he suffered, he was freed and given the second-highest position over all of Egypt. Not only that, but he forgave his brothers. "As for you, you meant evil against me, but God meant it for good, to bring it about that many people should be kept alive, as they are today." (Genesis 50:20)

No matter the giants lined up in battle against you, they will be slain. Your past is forgettable, and your future is surely livable. Remember Jesus' words to the young man? "Let the dead bury the dead..." Let your past be in your past. Look to the future. Trust in God's provision like Abraham did as he raised the knife over his son, Isaac. God will provide a ram, stuck in the bush.

Who has God called you to be? What truth is being revealed to you?

Are you ready to go deeper into areas of your brokenness? This very moment is the time to boldly declare, "Lord, I'm ready to go where you want to take me!" One of the first principles of transformation is it requires your personal decision to be intentional. You agree to God's transforming work by pressing into it on purpose.

REFLECTION

1. When you envision spiritual transformation in your life, in what ways are you different than you are right now?
2. Where is God breaking you and what trials have you faced?
3. What is God calling you to do that requires you to submit your will to his?

2

THE ENCOUNTER

The pattern of transformation always begins in the same way: with God's power and on his calendar (his timing). Our response to his work must be obedience. When we obey, transformation is underway.

When we intentionally run to Jesus with hunger and thirst, he responds immediately. Consider his words in Matthew 5:6: "Blessed are those who hunger and thirst for righteousness, for they shall be satisfied." He promises to satisfy those who ache for his will and work. Everyone who comes with an "I gotta have this" attitude is satisfied. When we seek Jesus, we find him with arms wide open ready to give resurrection power. He meets us in our desperation, in our need, and in our inadequacy.

Jesus does two things: he responds to our hunger and then reveals more. He is not a God of withholding; he is a God of giving. When you look to the cross, you see his outpouring of love and provision. What manner of love is this? How could his love ever be questioned? If he gave us Jesus, what would he possibly withhold? He first reveals that before all other things, he loves us. As we are transformed, he shows us that we are not called to perfect lives, but are welcomed in perfect love. Let this reality set your heart at rest. Have peace in his sovereignty. He is intentional toward us with his plan for our future.

This is where our encounter with Jesus begins: embracing his sovereignty and trusting in his power. Whatever is not right, he will make right. Whatever is broken, he will repair. Whatever is damaged, he will heal. Whenever we lose our way and need rescued, he's near. As Max Lucado says, "That's why they call him Savior." He's always saving us. Let this be the foundation for our obedience—that we can wholeheartedly trust in Jesus. I learned this first hand.

THE ANGELS

I left my home in Sioux Falls, South Dakota on a Friday night. I was taking my team, Barb and Iva, to the Indian reservation in Fort Thompson, South Dakota to do ministry. I had been going twice a week and this was my night to teach. But, before we ever set foot in Fort Thompson, something strange began to take place. The moment I stepped into the car, I felt like I was in heaven; in God's domain, in his space. Something supernatural happened to me, but I didn't know it until the women who were with me asked, "Are you okay?"

They knew something profound was happening. I told them, "I just had an encounter, an experience. It felt like I stepped into heaven."

They said, "You were talking to God and speaking other languages."

"I was?" I replied. I felt something stirring in me, and suddenly I knew what it was.

Immediately, I saw movement in the car like spouts of compacted air. They swirled and swooshed all around us. I was shocked! I exclaimed, "There's something strange happening. There are angels in this car!"

So I gave thanks for the angels who were with us and we continued on our way. When something like this happens, you know it is supernatural movement. I thought, "Wow, God's really going to show up tonight! We've got angels in the car already." We were 30 minutes down the road before I finally calmed down. What an experience this was; and I hadn't even started to preach yet. But the Lord did have plans to use us in a special way. Two supernatural things happened during the service in Fort Thompson that night.

THE DRUNK

First, a young man known as the town drunk came to the service. Everyone on the reservation knew him. He brought a good friend with him, who was a school teacher. That night, I was speaking about how God's power is greater than addiction's power to keep us in chains. About 15 minutes into my message, the drunk stood up and started walking down the aisle toward me. He was clearly inebriated—tall, with a solemn look on his face. As he came directly toward me, I continued speaking until he was just a few steps away.

He fell to his knees and put his head between his legs. Then he sat back up and cried, "I gotta have this power tonight!"

Right then I knew my sermon was over! I stepped to his side and prayed for him. As I did, his friend the school teacher came walking down the aisle and said, "I want it, too." I prayed for these men. After a short time, the drunk man stood up. His eyes were clear. He wasn't inebriated any longer, the drunkenness gone in the snap of a finger. The crowd looked at the now-sober man in stunned silence. The Holy Spirit had just intervened right before our eyes.

THE GIRL

Minutes after praying for the drunk man, I felt words being written on my heart and was compelled to say to the crowd, "I don't know who you are, but there is somebody in the back contemplating suicide and God has given me a message for you. The message is, 'Today is not the last day of your life, but the first day of a brand new life for you.'"

Suddenly, a young lady started to scream. She was brought to the front and knelt, sobbing. She looked at me and said, "That message was for me." Then, she pulled a bottle of pills from her purse and began saying, "I only came here tonight to ask the Lord to forgive me, because I was going to go home and kill myself."

Two lives were transformed that night. We were overjoyed at God's love upon that place. At the end of the meeting, we hugged, shook hands, and said goodbye in high spirits.

THE BULL

I rested in the back seat as we drove home. After we stopped for gas, I noticed Pastor Iva wasn't wearing her seatbelt. This was an unusual thing for me to notice. I constantly forget to wear my own seatbelt. But that night, I noticed and said, "Pastor Iva, put your seatbelt on." She just kept chatting away. So I pressed her again, "Pastor Iva, get your seatbelt on!" Then she looked at me, surprised, and said, "Okay, Pastor Judy. I'll put it on." Her seatbelt clicked in place. I laid down in the back seat with my head behind the driver's side, and fell asleep. Thirty minutes later as she was driving 75 miles per hour, our car came upon a black bull standing in the middle of the interstate. Iva was driving and couldn't see it until it was too late. *Bam!* We hit the bull and our car began to spin. Shattered glass flew everywhere from the impact and we crashed off the side of the road. The bull's blood was everywhere. The car was crumpled like a tin can, smashed on both sides. Miraculously, my two friends stepped out of the front seats without a single scratch. I, however, did not fare as well. Somehow, like a guided missile, the bull found his way to me.

My friends frantically tried to get to me. In the late-evening darkness, the car was so bowed from the collision that it was difficult to see anything. They finally reached me, cramped beneath the bent metal, and pulled me out. Pastor Iva was a nurse, Barb a physical education teacher. They checked my pulse and prayed over me. But their hearts fell. I had no pulse. They sobbed and wept together over my lifeless body, praying all the while, saying, "She's gone."

The women later told me that something incredible happened then. Even with no pulse, my body spoke, saying, "Stop crying, keep praying, because somebody's trying to take me out." It was a command straight from a dead woman's lips. In shock, they continued praying.

My entire face was mangled and bloody. My head was split open. I was completely unrecognizable. Once the ambulance arrived, they rushed me back to Sioux Falls, though I was still presumed dead. The paramedics said that had I been sitting up, I would have been decapitated. And if I had laid the opposite way, I would have been totally crushed. But something even more incredible happened that night.

THE VOICES

After I lost my life in that car, my spirit lifted from my body. I awoke in a smoky place, lying on my back. I looked up and saw a black cloud, rolling with death, moving toward me. First it engulfed my feet, crawling up my legs. Everywhere it touched, my body disappeared.

As it crept up to my waist, a calm, comforting voice said, "Judy, you've done well but your time is up. Come on home." The voice repeated itself, "Judy, you've done well. Your time is up. Come on home."

As the black cloud climbed higher, another voice rang out. Clear and authoritative. "No! Her time is not up."

Immediately, I knew that someone was trying to deceive me. I genuinely thought that the first voice was the Lord's. It was so calm and inviting. The second voice said again, "No! Her time is not up."

As soon as those words were spoken, the cloud folded back on itself and began receding. And as it receded, my body came back. In this instant, during this vision, I saw myself as a little girl in our old house. I saw my father's 1957 Buick. I saw myself jumping rope. Then I heard these words: "Whatever you have not done, it's too late. Wherever you have never gone, you'll never go, because this is it."

But those words came from the first voice. The voice that I now recognize as the deceiver's voice. You see, the deceiver twisted God's heavenly words from "Well done, good and faithful servant." to "You've done well, but it's time to come home." He said something so close to God's very words in Scripture. He mimicked his fatherly tone so well that I almost believed him. He used that language to woo me. The deceiver's heavenly tone sang a song of deception. But God's voice, the voice of truth, cut through the deception and saved me. However, the deceiver's lies wouldn't end there.

The cloud crawled down to the tip of my toes. I fell right back into my physical body and woke up in the hospital I'd been brought to by an ambulance. It was jarring and disorienting. I didn't know what I looked like, nor did I know the severity of my injuries. I woke up to the calming voice of Tom Rooney, my dear covenant brother, who rushed to the hospital the moment he heard about the accident. I remember him asking, "Pastor Judy do you remember where you were?" I vaguely remember him asking something about the reservation. Then, the next thing I heard was someone saying, "Call for a plastic surgeon." Just after this, I fell into a coma.

A few days later, I came out of the coma. I couldn't see and went through a period of blindness. I still didn't know what I looked like, or what had happened. I could feel that my face was not right. The doctors had put a layer of silicone over my face because of the trauma. As I healed, they prepared me to see a plastic surgeon because my face was so distorted.

When I was discharged, I couldn't go to my own house because of the many stairs, and my equilibrium was shot. So, I stayed at my father's single-level duplex. I lost my ability to recall names, I was unable to focus on anything without extreme pain—if I even looked at something for too long it felt like 2,000 stick pins were stuck into my head. When I went back to the doctor, I was still eating through a straw.

After a series of X-rays, my doctor said my face would require three reconstructive surgeries. He continued, "We'll need to take some skin from your legs and graft it, because you have next to no skin left on your face." He then asked me if I wanted to see myself, but seeing my mother's reaction, and my dear friend Doris' who had rushed to my side from Atlanta, GA, I declined.

After the surgeries, I was happy to finally be able to go home. But my plastic surgeon's assessment was not very comforting. Only then did the full weight of my injuries fall on me. Deceitful voices returned, offering a defeated verdict. They said, "Your ministry is over. Stay home and live as a recluse. You cannot possibly go out looking the way you do."

Lying in bed, I listened to them. And they whispered further, "The doctors will do some work on you, but those scars will never fade. The reason you won't go out is because everyone will feel sorry for you. But you don't want their pity, do you?" More twisted truth, intentionally spoken to keep me away from my intended destiny. If the deceiver could have convinced me to bite into that fruit of compromise, he would have shifted me away from the plan God already carved out for me. His plan and its outcome was far greater than the deceiver's. I just had to stick to his pattern.

I rolled up from my bed, tears welling in my eyes, and looked at myself in the bathroom mirror. I bought it. I believed they were right. My ministry, like my face, would be badly disfigured and contorted. People would only pity and tolerate me, and the gospel message would be minimized in their receiving. This was my momentary truth: I was a broken tool beyond repair, and my destiny was to live forgotten. These lies touched my mind, then seeped into my heart. And in that moment, looking at the lips that would never preach again, I believed the whispers that were stringing chords of vanity in my ears.

REFLECTION

1. How do you distinguish the different voices?
2. How can you better know the influence behind what's being said or done?
3. When have you mistaken the enemy's lies for God's truth?

3
THE LIES

When we believe lies, they gain the power to shape our lives. But, they only hold power over us if we agree with them. To agree with a lie is to believe and act on it as if it were true. This is when deception gains a foothold in our hearts.

In Romans 1:25, the Apostle Paul wrote about exchanging the truth of God for a lie. But what is a lie? What's its purpose? To answer this question, first bear with me a little folly and let me share a story.

One day in school, after hearing one of her pupils embellish the truth, the teacher decided to ask the student a question.

"Johnny, what is a lie?" she asked.

"Well that's easy, Ms. Johnson," he replied. "A lie is a very present help in the time of trouble!"

Now back to business! A lie is a false statement with intention to deceive. So what happens when we break free from lies we've believed? Our belief system changes. And when our beliefs change, so does the way we live. Dr. Wayne Dyer says, "Change your thoughts, change your life."

One of the most transforming books on the market today, written by Richard Flint, is *Behavior Never Lies*. Richard is considered a master on human behavior. I've sat in many of Richard's sessions and have had the pleasure of partnering with him in his conferences. In his book, truth strips you of every excuse and justification you've held onto. Then he carves out a path for you to take ownership, intentionally changing your behavior. He's another one of those "straight shooters" you need to have on your journey.

The night of my accident, coming from the reservation after that powerful session, I tumbled from the mountaintop into the valley. We saw lives turned around, hope restored, and people released from bondage. But after the car crash, all of that seemed to be over. I believed the lie that my injuries marked the end of my ministry and stole my destiny. Although I only believed this for a short time, it still held sway over me. I did what I call "buying the ticket." I came into agreement with a lie that had a destructive power and purpose for my life. A lie that contradicted my very purpose of living. A lie that blinded me to anything beyond my present state. Feeling a sense of helplessness and hopelessness, I agreed with the lie, shook its hand, and bought the ticket.

To make an agreement with something is to put our faith in it as if it were reality; it becomes your truth. Whether it's a lie or the truth, we're giving that idea complete control over an area of our lives. When we believe lies, we allow deception to reign in our hearts and minds. This means that our view of ourselves, of God, and of others becomes distorted. And this misshapen view of the world infects everything we do. We buy the ticket to a destination we can never arrive at—*because the train isn't really going where we're told it is.*

BUYING THE TICKET

For over twenty years, I have worked as a Spiritual Counselor with the Keystone Treatment Center in Canton, South Dakota, bringing healing and transformation to people's lives. Keystone is a place where miracles happen! Every single day, people learn how to break free from chains of bondage and are released from their fears as we endeavor to retool them for their journey to recovery. We purpose to give them a fresh, running start at life. In my work, there are common motifs I see among clients and their families. It doesn't matter if they are bankers, lawyers, or doctors—the sinister theme that unites them all is *deception*. They are bound by addiction because, at some point, they came into agreement with a lie.

In the spirituality classes I teach, I begin by saying, "Right now, you are not here because you are weak. You are here because you are strong. This is somewhat of an at-will facility, so any one of you could get up and leave at any time. But you have made a choice to stay, and for that I commend and applaud you." I simply tell them they're here because they have been deceived. As intelligent and strong-willed as they may be, the truth is they were tricked into buying a lie. The lie was, "It's just one hit." The lie was, "You can handle it," or "It's not that bad yet." You never bought this ticket to lose your reputation, your family, or your career. The truth turned out to be something much different. Now that the plane has landed here, the painful truth must be told. Truth is the master key needed to unlock the lie. Truth is light that dispels the darkness.

Buying the ticket is believing the lie. I allowed myself to believe that my ministry was over because of what happened to me in the accident. Though I know now that it was a deception, I didn't recognize it at first. Deception is twisted reality. It is a lie that promises one thing, yet delivers another. Deception's hidden poison is that it presents itself as the truth.

Intentionality is crucial here! This is the time you need the guts to expose yourself. You can't leave anything covered. You're required to revisit the pages of your life, and allow truth to reign where lies and deception have ruled. Transformation demands you dig deep so every lie is exposed and every motive reexamined so you can move into transformation.

THE POWER OF MAKING AN AGREEMENT

When we are faced with lies, we have a choice: will I agree with what is being presented to me, or not? You see, agreements give lies their power. To make an agreement is to say, "Yes, I believe that's where this ticket will take me." To agree with something is to align your life to it. And this is how we allow our lives to be shaped by either the truth or lies. From *Behavior Never Lies*, Richard says it like this: "Each day, a person only has two choices for that day of their life. They either choose to feed their confusion or strengthen their clarity."[1]

What we agree with, we become one with. We believe the lie, then we act it out. I remember my dad preaching about the life of Apostle Paul, whose name was Saul before his conversion to Christianity. Saul was a Roman citizen known to be a great persecutor. To be biblically accurate, he persecuted Christians. I listened to my father's attempt to explain Saul's behavior and his understanding. I realized he wasn't condoning his actions, but he did salute him for being true to his belief and conviction. In other words, he showed how Saul had believed a lie. He wholeheartedly believed that he was doing God's work. My dad said a lesson to be learned from Saul was this: "Be careful not to have your conscience educated with the wrong information." Words of wisdom from "my dad's vault."

We listen to other voices, embrace emotional thoughts, and then internalize them—like I did with the lie that my ministry was ruined. Just as some of my clients at Keystone believed that it was just one more hit, just one more drink, one more pill to pop, and then they would be done.

Our life really springs from our belief system. What we believe determines our actions. And when we make an agreement, there is an exchange that takes place—a sowing and reaping effect. In 1940,

---

[1]Flint, Richard. *Behavior Never Lies* (Kindle Locations 44–52). Flint Inc. 2008. Kindle Edition.

a popular radio program called *Truth or Consequences* quickly developed into a TV show that I remember watching when I was young. If the contestant's answer was wrong, they had a consequence to face. Remember Paul's words in Romans 6:23: "For the wages of sin is death, but the free gift of God is eternal life in Christ Jesus our Lord."

The only wage we can expect from sin is death. Wow! And who preaches that anymore? That's it. No matter how smooth or compelling the promise, if it's not of God, then it will end in death. However, when we trust in God's word, we are promised life. To agree with God is to say "yes" to what he says yes to, and "no" to what he says no to. Agreeing with him walks us right into our destiny because we're affirming that his will is our will, and his way is our way. This yokes us to Jesus, and we are led along the path of life. But when we agree with lies, we are yoked to the Adversary, and we walk a trail of bones to the graveyard. Remember Satan has his tactics, too.

RECOGNIZING THE SOURCE

So where does this leave us? This is the game changer for me. In my case, I thought the deceiver's voice was the voice of truth. It's very important we discern the source of whatever we are presented with. The first question we should ask then, is, "What nature is this decision appealing to?" Or, to keep with our analogy, "Who is selling me this ticket?" And there are only three possible answers: self, Satan, or Savior.

Most often, lies will appeal to our flesh. The Apostle John wrote, "For all that is in the world—the desires of the flesh and the desires of the eyes and pride of life—is not from the Father but is from the world." (1 John 2:16) The desires of the flesh, the desires of the eyes, and the pride of life form the great seduction. And when we follow our flesh, we are aligned with death. Here's the sobering reality: whoever makes your decisions now determines your destiny. A lie is a willful deception aimed at a destructive end. Jesus tells us that they are the offspring of the Father of Lies himself (John 8:44). So, what will it be for you: truth or consequences? You are in charge. You are the most valuable player in your life—and the ball is in your court.

BELIEVING THE TRUTH

Whom do you want determining your destiny: self, Satan, or Savior? If we pursue the passions of the flesh or the lies of the enemy, we can expect both spiritual and natural death. When we do this, we leave our legacy behind as Esau in the Bible did. We forfeit our God-given birthright, our spiritual inheritance. God's promises are always more than what we can achieve on our own.

If you examine your life and look closely at past trials, I am certain you will find this same pattern. When the storm comes, the enemy knows exactly what will terrify us most. He knows how to rock us and shake us when we are vulnerable. In these moments, we must hold to the most fundamental truth of them all: God is sovereign.

Remember the woman who suffered from bleeding for twelve years? She went from doctor to doctor, exhausting all her savings yet was never healed. But one hope remained. She heard that Jesus, the healer, was coming her way. She barely made her way to Jesus and had only enough strength to brush the fringe of his garment. But it was enough, because it was in that moment Jesus said, "Daughter, your faith has made you well; go in peace." (Luke 8:48) In an instant, her entire life was transformed. She was intentional in her pursuit for the only physician with the power to mend her broken body: Jesus himself. And her story of intentional transformation must become ours as well.

Amidst the lies, the struggles, and the uncertainties—right here, right now—reach out your hand and touch his garment. Get ready to have a Miracle Moment! I have to stop right now and join you, speaking over your life that your transformation begins this very moment. As you stretch out to grasp Jesus, he will respond to your touch, breathing new life into you. The slightest touch of your fingertips can make you well. Listen to the voice of your Heavenly Father, and have faith in him alone. Make an agreement in your heart to believe only things that are true. As my brother Willie always says, "Believe your beliefs and doubt your doubts. Don't make the mistake in believing your doubts and doubting your beliefs." And that is what the rest of this book is about: allowing truth to transform you.

REFLECTION

1. What lies have you made agreements with in your life? What false tickets have you bought?
2. Where in your life have you doubted the sovereignty of God?
3. Will you reach out in faith to touch Jesus like that bleeding sick woman did?

PART TWO

THE PATTERN

4

THE KINGDOM STRATEGY

God's Kingdom is his will and his way—and it is found wher-
ever Jesus is. The place of transformation is stretched out in
front of us, and the road to get there is always one of obedience.
As we are obedient, there is Kingdom power available to us to
accomplish God's purposes for our lives.

There is a pattern of transformation in God's Kingdom. Its secret is that it always begins and ends with him. When I looked at my broken face in the mirror, I did believe the lie that God's call on my life was finished—*but only for a moment* (and, by the way, you are allowed to have that human moment!). Then the pattern emerged and the Holy Spirit turned the lights on, as if I had been standing in a dark room. Through the entrance of light, truth revealed herself. The darkness that covered the lie was exposed! In an instant, I saw my trial for what it really was: the beginning of my transformation.

I looked at my bandaged face in the mirror and said, "Judy, you are more than a face and your anointing and giftedness are not found in your appearance! It doesn't matter how you look; God's power is still in you. You can do what he said you will do. And you will!" The Lord gently revealed the vanity and pride the enemy took up as a weapon against me. He showed me what was true and revealed the deception for what it was. I resolved that even though I may look like Zoro had just slashed me, I'm still going to speak and pursue God's call.

Then, after this internal transformation took place, I began to experience miraculous physical changes as well. In the weeks that followed, my skin regenerated and healed itself at an unbelievably rapid rate that could only point to God's divine healing power. With each appointment, the plastic surgeon pushed back the reconstructive surgery. He delayed the skin grafts and stood in awe at my recovery. The Lord was making me new from the inside out. To this day, I praise him because I made a full physical recovery without the surgeon's scalpel. This is my testimony to God's healing power and his nearness. I reached and brushed the hem of his robe. I held onto his truth, and was healed in a way no physician could have matched. No scars, no blemishes—smooth skin that's a daily reminder of God's power.

Now, excuse me while I take a praise break!

"As we let our own light shine, we unconsciously give other people permission to do the same."

Marianne Williamson

YOUR MARCHING ORDERS

I'd like to share a wonderful and unexpected conversation I had with another dear friend of the family, Mrs. Barbara McCoo-Lewis. We both hailed from the great state of Texas and had known each other for years. She had always been like a big sister to me. But even more, she was an influential and highly-respected woman of God.

Barbara called, concerned about my well-being and recovery. By then, everyone had heard the news of the accident. It was publicly broadcasted in one of the largest international women's conferences that year held by the Church of God in Christ called "The Women's International Convention." As Barbara and I spoke, she encouraged me. But it also became evident she was on a mission. She proved to be my Mordecai. Actually, she gave me my marching orders.

Even though I was hurt, she challenged me to keep moving. I needed that! Like a general giving a strategic plan, she told me to set a goal date for when I would step back into ministry. She emphasized the importance of getting over the fear of returning. And in a single conversation, she strengthened me, reaffirmed my calling, and locked me into being the speaker at her annual women's conference in southern California, which would have about 5,000 women in attendance.

I must admit, I thought it was way too soon. But I trusted my friend and her wisdom. I trusted the voice of God in her and replied with an immediate, "Yes!" Two months later, with the bandages on my forehead hidden beneath a scarf, I went to California, stepped into that huge auditorium, and did what I doubted I was ready to do. And it was glorious.

You see, Barbara was part of my transformation community at that time. Because she was intentional, I too became intentional. You will always have situations in your life when you'll need a Barbara to give you clear instructions to jump start you again. That step of action replaced my fear. And for that, I'm eternally grateful.

THE KINGDOM PRINCIPLES

When God transforms us, we become more like Jesus. That is the ultimate destiny for every one of us, to be conformed to Jesus' image. Looking like Jesus, walking like Jesus, talking like Jesus, living like Jesus, acting like Jesus, and lastly, loving like Jesus. This is Kingdom reality. I had watched, witnessed, and have been deceived for many years into thinking that the kingdom of man was the Kingdom of God. Each has its own principles, powers, agendas, and modes of operation. Scripture foreshadows this truth in 2 Samuel 3:1: "The war between the house of Saul and house of David lasted a long time. The house of David grew stronger and stronger, while the house of Saul grew weaker and weaker." These two kingdoms on the earth are at odds. Saul's kingdom represents the kingdom of man, while David's kingdom represents the Kingdom of God. One grew stronger while the other grew weaker. One is clothed in man's glory, and the other robed with God's glory. One is temporary, and the other is eternal. Can you hear the heavenly host singing, "And He shall reign forever and ever…?" I can.

Jesus' desire for us is to be one with him as he and the Father are one. And it simply looks like this: his plan, his way, and in his time.

If Jesus is in you, so is the Kingdom. It is heaven's reign in our hearts in spite of the strongholds that govern the kingdom of man. To walk the Kingdom path is to honor and obey the King. Obedience is the hallmark of God's people. For me, stepping back into the pulpit was an act of obedience to God and of defiance against hell. Everywhere I go, I have fun as I boldly announce, "If you have never seen, touched, or felt the Kingdom of Heaven, come touch my hand, my face… I am the Kingdom manifested!"

Walking by Faith

Obedience is the fruit of absolute trust in God. It is trusting more in what he has said than in what you can see. It is believing and agreeing with his words from Scripture. And as you do, a clearer understanding of God's nature, character, and faithfulness emerges. We are deepened when we depend on God more than ourselves. When we trust him, there is greater revelation of the Kingdom. It's the ultimate *rest*.

Knowing the Word

Fundamental to trusting God, however, is knowing his word. How can you trust him if you don't know what he has promised? God's word reveals to us who God is and who we are. It shows us his law, his will, and his way. It puts on full display his tenderness, mercy, and love. We see God faithfully acting on behalf of his people from

Genesis all the way to Revelation. We read of promise after promise fulfilled. But if we aren't intimately familiar with his word, how can we know him—much less trust him? And if we don't have knowledge of his word, we don't know who we are, either.

The word is both letter and spirit. As we read the word, our mind acts like an information center. Our brain collects data and files it away. But there's no saving belief that comes from your mind alone. Saving faith resides in our hearts. That is why the word is also spirit. As we read it, listen to it, or hear it taught, the Holy Spirit brings the words to life within us. And not the Spirit only, but Jesus himself.

God inspired men to write down his words—what was spirit became physical. In John 1, we read that Jesus himself is *the* Word, the *logos*. So not only are we students of the written word, we are disciples of the Word incarnate. Jesus, the King of Kings, "became flesh and dwelt among us." (John 1:14) Just as Jesus took on flesh, the words of God took on ink. As we are made more like Jesus—the Word—we become living epistles. We embody his truth, carry his light, impart his life, and release his love as God's Kingdom agents sojourning among the kingdom of man.

Acting on the Word

To embody God's word simply means to act on it. The Kingdom advances as we are obedient to his call. As his messengers, we don't only learn and memorize his words; we live them out!

As his word springs to life in us, it overflows into how we think, feel, and act. James put it perfectly, that "faith without works is dead." (Jas 2:26) So our faith in God is shown to be alive by our obedience to his commands.

Remember the persistent widow? She begged and pleaded, day after day, with the unrighteous judge who "neither feared God nor respected man." (Luke 18:2) She cried out for justice; he refused. She asked again; he refused. So she persisted again and again, until finally he relented, saying, "Though I neither fear God nor respect man, yet because this widow keeps bothering me, I will give her justice, so that she will not beat me down by her continual coming." (Luke 18:4-5) In this parable, Jesus shows us what persistent, expectant, and dynamic faith looks like. The widow wouldn't stop seeking justice, even from an unrighteous judge.

Is God righteous or unrighteous? He's righteous, of course! So if this woman had the faith to come before the earthly judge, how much more faith should we have in our heavenly Father? And that faith should provoke us to action. The kind of action that Jude described, that contends, "for the faith that was once for all delivered to the saints." (Jude 1:3) It is an overcoming faith that wants to get to Jesus at all costs. It was delivered *unto* the saints and it *delivered* the saints.

This is the kind of faith that led men to cut a hole in a roof to get their friend to Jesus. It's the kind of faith that moved a very sick woman's hand to touch the hem of Jesus' robe. It's the faith that says to the mountain, "Get up and throw yourself into the sea," with the conviction that it will be done. This is the faith that gave birth to the

New Testament church. This is faith that can be seen. Faith without evidence is no faith at all. Because "faith is the assurance of things hoped for" and "the conviction of things not seen." (Heb 11:1) Faith has evidence, faith has results, faith has proof! What is your faith in?

KINGDOM POWER

Active faith is powerful faith. But it requires a resolve because we are not operating as God's Kingdom people without opposition. We face an enemy—a devious lion, never satisfied, constantly roaring in hunger, on the hunt for his next meal. And when we operate in this kind of faith, that lion wants us on his menu.

This is the deal! Until Jesus returns, we will always be a people at war. There will always be opposition to face and giants to slay. Just as God had stretched out new life in front of me, you too have a place of awakening ahead—a place where you will be transformed. There will always be opposing giants who want to keep you from that place. We, however, are not without the power to tear down and destroy their influence.

What Does This Power Look Like?

Man does the natural; God does the supernatural. Man does the ordinary; God does extraordinary. Man does the possible; God does the impossible. Kingdom power comes from the Scripture, which is "breathed out by God and profitable for teaching, for reproof, for correction, and for training in righteousness, that the man of God may be complete, equipped for every good work." (2 Tim 3:16-17)

Just like a soldier is equipped for battle, we are equipped for obedience. It's in our DNA. But if we don't do our part, if we don't take action, why does God have to equip us? As we are faithful, he gives us the power we need to accomplish his purposes. This means supernatural power. People are healed, strongholds are broken, dead hearts are brought to life. This means resurrection power. The same hand that resurrected Jesus from the grave is strengthening us as well.

Ladies and gentlemen: this is who we are and this is what we do!

This all begins with our desire to see his will accomplished. I have an insatiable desire to see his Kingdom manifested in the earth. I yearn to see God fulfill his precious promises to his people. It's time for "Thy will be done, on earth as it is in heaven." We must desire to experience the full release of his Kingdom on earth as it is in heaven. His desire must become our desire, and his expectation must be our expectation. God will have a glorious church, a beautiful bride to showcase as his glory. Before us is a heavenly vision to follow and obey. When we do, we will experience this Kingdom power firsthand. First and foremost, it is personal. It has its own internal motivations. It is uninterrupted, possessing an absolute resolve. And there is no such thing as a third-party referral system. Only your passion and pursuit will give you a testimony of unbelievable transformation.

REFLECTION

1. Where does the Kingdom pattern of transformation begin?
2. Whose Kingdom are you loyal to? Where do you draw the line?
3. Where are you being called to obey? What's your next move?

5

THE ENEMY'S STRATEGY

Just like the Kingdom strategy, the enemy has a strategy as well—and it's an all-out war on intentional transformation. He twists reality and presents deception as truth. This is an uncomfortable conversation for many of us. But we ignore Satan's destructive work and tactics at our own peril. Instead, we can expose his pattern of deceit and recognize it each and every time.

Intentional transformation breeds resistance.

Your enemies and mine are the enemies of God. Since the beginning, they have stood in opposition to God's plan, which is to see us transformed into the image of Jesus (Rom 8:29). They are always trying to unweave his grand tapestry of redemption. Lucifer was a worship leader in heaven until pride consumed him, and he tried to set his throne above God's. And those angels who fell with him are still trying to establish his kingdom over heaven's. Our enemy, who was manifested as a serpent in the garden, still slithers in our midst. But because of his treachery, God set enmity between he and Eve, between his offspring and hers (Gen 3:15). Jesus, the heir and new Adam, did indeed crush his head. However, the enemy bruised his heel.

From the moment Jesus was born, Satan sought to see him killed. The ultimate power had come. The highest form of authority was now on the earth. Satan was not clueless; he knew the deal, and he still does. He knows what he has is not legit! To the believer, it is illegitimate authority. Believe that! When Jesus shows up, Satan knows his days are numbered. He plots, he plans, he huffs and he puffs, but he will never be able to blow Jesus' house down. "On this rock, I will build my church, and the gates of [hell] shall not overcome it." (Matt 16:18) The enemy worked through Herod. He inflicted a massacre of innocents in the Bethlehem region, where every boy under three years of age was to be killed (Matt 2:16). But Joseph and Mary carried the infant Christ to safety after being warned of this plot in a dream (Matt 2:12). Jesus' life was saved by heaven's intervention, and hell's forces were pressed back. But the enemy did not give up.

When Jesus began his ministry, the serpent's lies were resurrected. While fasting for forty days in the wilderness, Satan tempted him three times (Matt 4). Remember the challenge of his identity as the Son of God: "If you are who you say you are, turn these stones into loaves of bread." And the second challenge of his sonship from the pinnacle of the temple: "If you are God's son, throw yourself down and let the angels catch you." And the grand promise of immediate praise and kingship in all the nations of the world: "Bow down and worship me, and all of this can be yours."

Most cunning of all, however, was the betrayal of Judas at the end of Jesus' earthly ministry (Matt 26:15). For thirty pieces of silver, Judas handed Jesus to the people who would falsely accuse and then murder him on the cross. All of this under the direct influence of Satan (Luke 22:3). But, of course, we know that Jesus won that day, and by his stripes we are healed (Isa 53:5).

Again, do you see the strategy and pattern? From the garden to the manger to the cross, Satan is constantly working to thwart God's master plan of salvation. Everything he does is to prevent people from experiencing eternal life with God. He wooed Eve in Eden. He perverted God's own words to tempt the Word himself in the wilderness. And he sent the Savior to the cross. Everything Satan does is an effort to depose God from his throne and exalt himself. This is the enemy's pattern: *take what God has meant for good and twist it to kill people and glorify himself.*

In John 10:10, Satan is called a thief. While Jesus came to give us abundant life, Satan's mission is to steal that life—to destroy us before we can ever live out our God-given promise. A thief's plan is always hidden, unannounced, strategically organized, and out to take possession of its object for keeps. A thief can only be a thief when he takes what does not belong to him. He goes after what's valuable, what's forbidden to him, and takes pleasure in trying to undermine God's plan. His every move is an illegal transaction on the earth, and his authority is illegitimate.

For many of us, this is an uncomfortable conversation. But it is a crucial one if you want to encounter the real Jesus who hung on the cross, not a mere image of the one who hangs on our walls. Don't unintentionally buy into a contract to neglect your life's purpose. If you ignore the reality of our enemy, you're in agreement with his plans to lull the Church to sleep. But I prophesy that the sleepy giant, the Church, is awakening—renewing her mind, putting on beautiful garments, shining with his glory, walking in resurrection power, and standing boldly with his authority. She is declaring the day of the Lord, setting captives free, binding up the broken-hearted, strengthening her weak, healing her wounded, executing the vengeance of the Lord, carrying a two-edged sword, singing his high praises, proclaiming, "Our God reigns!"

If you belong to Jesus, you participate in this war whether you want to or not. If you choose to believe it's not happening, that doesn't make it true. The enemy follows the same process and pattern again and again. In this chapter, I want to expose him and his tactics. The snares he uses to trap us. The fiery arrows he shoots to wound us. After all, deceitful as he is, we are not ignorant of his schemes (2 Cor 2:11). Have you ever noticed patterns in your family line? Has alcoholism or violence gone on for generations? Have addictions been a constant part of your family? Do you see the strategy?

He's intentionally at war against God's redeeming work in people. And he sends his generals and commanders against us, not simply privates and recruits (Luke 11:24-26). Transformation breaks chains. Transformation destroys strongholds. But it is a battle to fight. The total and complete change God works in us happens through this war. It happens as we slay the giants before us. And as we learned last chapter, we have Kingdom power to wage this fight. But before we ever strike our first blows, we must wake up to the reality that we live in a Kingdom at war every moment of every day.

THE ENEMY'S WEAPONS OF WAR

God's enemies work in a predictable pattern. On the night of my accident, Satan's voice was a comforting melody to me: "Judy, you've done well. It's time to come home." The pattern always begins with a distortion of the truth. This is why Paul warned the Corinthians that Satan wears the disguise of an angel of light (2 Cor 11:4). Then, if we buy into his sugary-sweet lies, he causes us to live below our privilege. He lowers the standard God has set for us. Then suddenly, we're being led away from the straight and narrow trail the Holy Spirit has blazed for us.

The enemy's game plan is always based on deception. So we must always have a mindset that says, "I only have one truth: God's truth. I only have one identity: as a son or daughter of God." This view of reality begins by understanding his means of deception. And in my experience, the enemy uses six strategies to fight God's transforming work in us: *distraction, promoting self-focus, twisting God's plans, faces of doubt, faces of fear, and the many faces of shame.* They are so subtle that if we aren't alert to the reality that we live in a battle zone, it's easy to wander from God's transformation in us.

Distraction

The first weapon in the enemy's arsenal is distraction. Distraction is losing sight of God's plan. This comes in many forms. It's a prime tactic used against us. That's why Paul said that the "god of this world has blinded the minds of the unbelievers, to keep them from seeing the light of the gospel of the glory of Christ, who is the image of God." (2 Cor 4:4)

Two key things are happening here. First, just like unbelievers, we become blinded by what the world offers. We focus on money or getting praised by people. This makes us lose focus on storing up treasures in heaven. It makes us forget our Father's approval. Our blindness makes us stumble because we aren't seeing with God's vision any longer. We let ourselves become a part of a system that's not God's system (Rom 12:2). At its core, this is idolatry. We are worshiping creation rather than the Creator.

The second thing that's happening is that we lose sight of Jesus himself. And what is God transforming us into? Jesus' image! So if we don't have our eyes on Jesus, how can we follow him? How can we do what he does? Love what he loves? Pursue what he is pursuing? How can we become like him if we've lost sight of him? We can't. Distraction is an effective weapon of the enemy because it keeps people from the gospel. It also keeps us, as God's children, from seeing the world through a spiritual lens. And instead, we adopt the world's mentality.

Promoting Self-Focus

The second weapon of the enemy is related to the first, but is worth detailing in its own right. Satan always tries to promote a self-focus in us. This form of distraction is the easiest to fall for, but one of the hardest to see. He comes at us from every angle.

He promotes pride and self-love. And yet he also promotes shame and self-hate. He pushes us to self-promotion, and then pulls us into false humility—which is very common in the church. People who are transformed look to Jesus for their identity. But people who find themselves in the same place again and again, with no fruit of transformation, are usually stuck on themselves. We forget the alphabet starts with *A* and not *I*.

I want to challenge you here, because this is a choice. Are you stuck in an orbit of self-focus? Are you constantly thinking about yourself before other people? Is your comfort the primary motive for your life? Are you willing to risk being uncomfortable to be obedient? If so, you are following God's pattern of transformation. If not, you're succumbing to the enemy's. But be encouraged, because this is a choice you can make. Choose transformation and focus on the Lord.

Twisting God's Plans

We looked at how Satan tried to twist God's plans in Jesus' ministry earlier in this chapter. But now I want to take a look at how he does this in our lives. The first place he twists God's plans in our life is by pulling us onto an easier path. He shows us shortcuts, just like he did to Jesus. He makes us believe that there are easier options than picking up our crosses every day. But this isn't true.

When this happens, you might have the chance to get a little more recognition. And all he has to do is give us a nudge, then let our flesh take care of the rest. This is why James wrote that, "each person is tempted when he is lured and enticed by his own desire." (James 1:14) So, what do you want more: what God wants, or what you want? Are you after God's perfect will, or your comfortable will? Are you looking to be transformed through trials, or avoid them? Avoiding trails and pain is avoiding personal growth. Progress comes through process. Prepare yourself, and plan to follow the process. The Apostle Paul tried to give them a new perspective on life's vicissitudes. He said, "Think it not strange when these trials come upon you…"; "Arm yourself…"; "Endure hardness like a good soldier…"; "Fight the good fight of faith…"

What did Paul tell the Ephesians to do? Three things: *Put off the old self, put on the new self, and wear the full armor of God*. We'll take a deeper look at the armor of God in the next chapter. But putting off the old self and putting on the new self are important ideas. In Ephesians 4:22-24, Paul explains that the old self "belongs to your former manner of life and is corrupt through deceitful desires." He's agreeing with James here. Our old nature gets twisted up, and the enemy uses it to get us off-kilter. We lose our balance, so to speak. We stumble from God's way and walk in our own—which is really the enemy's. So what can we do?

Next, Paul tells us to put on the new self, "created after the likeness of God in true righteousness and holiness." Are you seeing the theme of transformation here? Our new self is a transformed self. It's a renewed mind and heart that turns our faith into action. The new life God works in us is created after his image—that's the Kingdom pattern. "And we all, with unveiled face, beholding the glory of the Lord, are being transformed into the same image from one degree of glory to another. For this comes for the Lord who is the Spirit." (2 Cor 3:18a)

Faces of Doubt

The first three weapons of the enemy are closely related, and so are the last three we will discuss. But more than simply weapons, I like to look at these as faces. They are the faces of doubt, fear, and shame. There are so many ways that these faces surface in our lives. There are many shapes and forms, but behind each mask is the same enemy with the same purpose: to kill, steal, and destroy (John 10:10).

In my life, the face of doubt often causes me to deliberate. I slow down and overanalyze things. I'm not saying that God's will is that we mindlessly rush ahead. However, there is a time for reflection, planning, and careful consideration. But there is also a time to act in faith, even if we don't see the full picture. This is what my friend Barbara McCoo-Lewis helped me with. This is what it means to trust the Lord with our whole hearts, rather than lean on our own understanding (Prov 3:5). And this is also what it looks like to hold to David's words in Psalm 37:23-24: "The steps of a man are established by the LORD, when he delights in his way; though he fall, he shall not be cast headlong, for the LORD upholds his hand."

Yes, we may stumble. But remember: whose power we are operating in? Whose authority are we given to walk in? Because it is God's work, it is only by his hand that it can be accomplished.

Here's the point: *his plans do not fall through if we don't come through; but he does invite us to partner with him in accomplishing them.* Doubt is a form of unbelief, so when we allow it to gain a foothold, we are taking our eyes off of the Lord and allowing the enemy to slow us down—and sometimes, to stop all together. The faces of doubt gain control over us when we make an agreement with the deception that God is counting on us to get everything right. Do you see what the root of this thinking is? Pride.

The Faces of Fear

Pride is the sickly root from which forests of blighted trees grow. It infects almost everything we do. And it doesn't only play a role in doubt, it brings fear bubbling to the surface as well. Fear has been nearly constant in my life—and most of the time, without me being aware of it. It's been one of the toughest giants I've had to fight. In fact, it used to stop me dead in my tracks. I was so afraid of what people thought of me that sometimes it paralyzed me. I allowed that fear to control me, to keep me quiet and locked up. But as I better understood God's perfect love—and learned to accept it—I grew stronger. Fear is not evaporated. Sometimes it still rears its ugly head. But now, instead of letting it bind me, if necessary, I drag it along with me. I move no matter what! I give my apprehension over to our God who is love. And what does God's perfect love do?

The Apostle John gives us the answer: "There is no fear in love, but perfect love casts out fear. For fear has to do with punishment, and whoever fears has not been perfected in love." (1 John 4:18) Perfect love casts out fear. When we understand the complete and total love God has for us, there is no more room for fear. Fear is pushed out of the window. In the Father's love, there is a "no vacancy" sign flashing above our hearts.

One of my favorite illustrations when I'm preaching is to ask the question, "How many people have been saved once?" Nearly everyone in the congregation will raise their hands. Then I say, "Well, now it's going to be twice. Today is your second salvation. It is a salvation from the fear of man." Many of us are immobilized by our fear of what other people will think or say about us. We don't step out and step up. We stay in the pew with the rest of the crowd, hoping that we escape criticism. Do you wonder how I know this? It's because I've lived it.

When I first began my ministry in Sioux Falls, I was "welcomed" into the community by the pastor of an established church. He told me that people were only coming to my church because I was "the new charismatic face on the block," and soon the novelty would "wear off." He said that I wouldn't last in this town. I've had countless experiences like this in ministry. "We don't believe in women pastors…", "You are a single pastor, you won't make it…", "This city is not ready for an Afro-American pastor…", "You are divorced; your credibility is on the line…", "You are way too friendly…", "You are from the city, your culture is different…", and the list goes on! But now I see the pattern. Today, I'm wise to the enemy's tricks. When things like this happen, I realize he's trying to weaponize the fear of failure in me. And most heinous of all, he's done so while wearing the mask of other people in the church. Remember, perfect love casts out fear. It doesn't matter what kind of fear it is. If it's not fear of God alone, then it is not from him.

Faces of Shame

The final mask we'll address is the face of shame. The face of shame doesn't simply say, "You've done bad things." It says, "You're bad, down to the very core." For the first ten years in my ministry, I had a hard time forgiving myself for my shortcomings. Everything was black and white. I was so hard on myself that no matter what I did, a sense of shame constantly bubbled beneath the surface of my life. And that's the deception. The lie is that even though you are in Christ, his grace isn't sufficient for you. It's enough for everyone else, but not for you. Shame is self-induced. Nobody can cause shame in you. You carry it. You own it. It's self-inflicted.

Now, this shouldn't be a shocking revelation. But if we uproot that weed, what will we find? We see pride working within us again. Shame is a perverse, camouflaged form of pride because it leads you to believe that your sin is greater than God's grace. It stacks up the wrong you've done and says, "This mountain of sin stands taller than the power of the cross." In effect, you're buying the lie that Jesus' goodness is weaker than your badness. But that isn't true! Your shame should melt away when you hold on to the power of the cross. When you encounter Jesus, you understand that he's the ultimate authority, he's the judge, he's the one who broke down hell's gates and took the keys. When God looks at you, he sees Jesus—not a mountain of sin.

My father used to tell me that, "Judy, you can't be as hard on people as you are on yourself. You try to live angelic holiness, but you need to live human holiness! You're a woman, not an angel. You are flesh and blood." At first, I didn't get it. But as I grew in the Lord, I saw that we can never be without sin. Even better, our sin is never greater than the cross. It's not about a perfect life, it's about his perfect love. We will always experience human judgment, but God's judgment is the one that counts. The blood of Jesus washes us clean and the judge of all the earth declares us righteous.

THE WAR ROOM

The six weapons catalogued in this chapter are always being hurled and swung at us. The enemy is constantly setting traps and snares to trip us up. And the chief war room is our minds. Your mind is the primary battleground where you will fight, because it is where we separate truth from lies. We make agreements with either fact or falsehood every single day. So we must dismantle deception to remember what reality is. Our minds are the proving ground where we decide to walk in the Spirit or in the flesh. This is why Paul warned the Romans: "Do not be conformed to this world, but be transformed by the renewal of your mind, that by testing you may discern what is the will of God, what is good and acceptable and perfect." (Rom 12:2)

You must be the gatekeeper of your mind, because it is the gateway to your heart. And whatever holds our heart is in control of our destiny. This is what the enemy fights for: *to disengage you from your destiny*. His weapons are designed to steal your sight, stop your ears, and make you lame. They are a flurry of confusion and distraction, all to keep us separated from God's plan for your life. You cannot ignore the battle. You cannot neglect staying alert for the pattern of the enemy. It's time to open your eyes for the sake of your own legacy and generation.

So what does that look like? First, remember that God has already purchased you from the kingdom of darkness and won the victory. You must walk beneath that banner. He has not left you without Kingdom power; you have heaven's arsenal at the ready. Now, all you have to do is use it.

REFLECTION

1. Which weapon does the enemy use most effectively against you?
2. How can you better recognize his pattern in your life?
3. Do you guard your "war room" with the understanding that what you believe is internalized into your heart?

PART THREE

THE POWER

6
THE RESOLVE

The Lord has provided us with a spiritual armory to wage the battle we are surrounded by. But these weapons and defenses are only effective if we put them to use.

Paul described the nature of our battle to the church in Ephesus. He said that we face an enemy who is always scheming. Every moment of every day, he's prodding and poking at us, trying to find a way in. He's always looking for the chink in our armor so he can wound us in some way. But our battle is not against flesh and blood, is it? It's against "the rulers, against the authorities, against the cosmic powers over this present darkness, against the spiritual forces of evil in the heavenly places." (Eph 6:12)

We are faced with an invisible onslaught that would completely overwhelm us if it wasn't for this, that we can "be strong in the Lord and in the strength of his might," and put on "the whole armor of God." (Eph 6:10-18 paraphrased) We are equipped to defeat the enemies that rule from dark, spiritual hideouts. But before we even talk about our spiritual battle armor and weapons, we must *receive them*. These promises of strength are ours in the Lord, but until we *put them on*, they won't do us any good. Have you allowed yourself to receive what God has given you?

To discern this, ask yourself these questions and answer honestly:

- Do you renew your mind to agree only with God's truth, rather than be deceived?
- Do you believe that, in Jesus, you are made righteous?
- Do you have a hunger to share the gospel?
- Do you have an ever-increasing faith that God is who he says he is, and will do what he has said he will do?
- Do you accept his free gift of salvation and grace?
- Do you have a fervent prayer life because you believe God hears, answers, and is moved by it?

If you are like me, at times you will be able to answer "yes" to many of these questions. But at other times in your life, the honest answer is, "no." The purpose of this chapter is to remind you that you have already been equipped and given victory in the Lord. But you must receive it through faith.

BUILDING FAITH

You may have noticed that each of the six questions above corresponds to what Paul calls the "whole armor of God." I have heard great teaching on our heavenly battle gear many times. You probably have, too. But I want to look at God's soldiers from a different perspective. We all know that we should put this armor on—but have you ever noticed that once it's on, we have the tendency to take it off?

To build our faith is to have the resolve to leave our armor on. To hold our shield steady and keep our sword ready. It's a Kingdom mindset that participates with the Spirit. It's having the mind of Christ, and Joshua's attitude that, "As for me and my house, we will serve the Lord." (Josh 24:15) It's repeating after Esther, "If I perish, I perish." (Esth 4:16) When we resolve to serve the Lord alone, we come to the ultimate conclusion that we are all in, no matter what. There is no wavering and no room for double-mindedness. To be resolved is a mark of a mature believer, one who is established and settled.

THE WHOLE ARMOR OF GOD

The whole armor of God is a combination of six tools for spiritual offense and defense. It enables us to attack, to defend, and to stay secure. Our minds, our hearts, and our bodies are protected. And we have the spiritual weapons necessary to strike blows against the powers and principalities that we're at war with. Paul tells us that the armor is:

1. The belt of truth;
2. The breastplate of righteousness:

3. The shoes ready to share the gospel of peace;
4. The shield of faith;
5. The helmet of salvation;
6. And the sword of the Spirit.

Each item is unique and a necessary part of the whole. Every day, we can do an "armor check." We can pray, "Lord, is my armor on? Is my mind renewed? Have I received the power you've given me to accomplish your will and destiny for my life?" We start with Course #101: renewed minds and hearts that long for God's purpose to be done. This is the mindset of a Kingdom warrior: *to see the will of the King accomplished.*

You know you are ready for Course #102 when your prayer sounds like this:

"Lord, I thank you for the armor you have given me. I am armed and dangerous, walking in faith and victory, declaring, 'Today, no weapon formed against me shall prosper.' Declaring, 'I have power over the enemy and nothing shall harm me. I am ready for battle!' You have taught my hands to war, I have the mind of Christ, and I will overcome. In the name of Jesus the gates of hell shall not prevail against me!"

As I said before, however, we sometimes take our armor off or leave our sword in its sheath. So let's walk through each piece, one by one, and examine how we take each off. How do we charge the battlefield with our sword on the shelf? When do we leave our helmet of salvation on the shelf? And what does it look like if this becomes a rhythm, or pattern, in our spiritual walk? What do we leave ourselves vulnerable to?

The Belt of Truth

Imagine a knight riding to battle on a horse. Can you see the helm? Do you see the sword flashing in the sun? The breastplate gleaming? The shield raised, ready for anything the enemy can throw at it? Now, when you picture this armor-clad warrior, what don't you focus on? The belt, right? When someone says the word "knight", your first association is likely not a belt. But there is a definite reason why Paul started here.

The belt of truth is a central piece of armor because, without it, the rest of the armor falls apart. In the first century, a soldier's belt was the piece that held everything else together. Without it, the breastplate would rattle off and the sword had nowhere to be held. And this is just as powerful a metaphor in the spiritual realm. Just like a soldier's belt, it is God's truth that holds everything together.

Without truth, we are unprotected and susceptible to believing anything. Without truth, the enemy can win our mind—and from there, the battle. When we remove the belt of truth we are open to spiritual injury. This is when erroneous doctrines take hold and heresy takes up residence in your heart and head. Truth keeps us grounded in the word. And one of the chief truths is, "He loves me." As a matter of fact, he's absolutely crazy about me!

Remember Paul's question to the Galatians: "Who has bewitched you?" (Gal 3:1) He was making the case that we are only justified by faith, and not works of the law. But they had bought into a perverted gospel that taught one needed Jesus plus certain works of righteousness to be saved. But their equation was off, wasn't it? It's not Jesus plus anything—it's Jesus and him alone.

We also take off the belt of truth when we compromise and justify our sin. Have you ever done this? Have you ever rationalized your way around repenting of certain sin? This, again, is a deception. It's the easy way out to get what we want instead of what God intends. But James gives us the truth about purity. Pure religion is this: "to visit orphans and widows in their affliction and to keep oneself unstained from the world." (James 1:27b) Pure Christianity is witnessed in faith that overflows into works of love and a life that's set apart from the kingdom of the world. As Christians, we neither love nor live like the world. But when we let the belt of truth slip from around our hips, compromise will inevitably take its place.

If you're wondering if you've done this—or are doing it right now—ask yourself these two questions: "What has more influence in my life: the world or the word?" and, "Whom do I most aspire to be like: Jesus or the culture I'm surrounded by?" If the answer is not the word and Christ, then the belt of truth has fallen. But do you know what? The amazing part is that you can pick it right back up and clasp it on. No matter when or where we wander, just like the father who welcomed the prodigal son home, God welcomes us home. This is truth, and it is to God's glory. He is a good Father and loves us as his own.

Shoes of the Gospel of Peace

Related to the questions we just asked are the shoes prepared for our feet. These gospel shoes are our evangelism readiness. Shoes mean travel. They mean protection for feet over rocky ground, burning sand, or frigid waters. Shoes both protect and propel us. And the shoes ready to share the gospel of peace do that, and so much more. Not only do they offer protection to us, they bear the good news of healing to the nations. They enter every tribe and tongue across the globe. There is no place these shoes will not carry us.

As Christians, we were made to move. Jesus sent the disciples out two by two, and gave his final commission to, "Go therefore and make disciples of all nations, baptizing them in the name of the Father and of the Son and of the Holy Spirit, teaching them to observe all that I have commanded you. And behold, I am with you always, even to the end of the age." (Matt 28:19-20) Unfortunately, we often take these shoes off because we have no intention of going.

Are you ready to share the gospel? When we have really encountered Christ, there is a burden to share this experience. Look to the woman at the well in John 4. She ran back to her village of Sychar and invited everyone, "Come with me and meet a man who told me everything I ever did!" (John 4:29) When we know God, we seek to make him known. These shoes were hand-crafted for children of the promise. And they are promised to be accompanied by Jesus himself even "to the end of the age."

We take them off when we are distracted by the cares of the world. The enemy uses tools to enamor and entice us away: money, sex, power, safety, comfort, security, fame, gluttony—the list is endless. These sap our desire to be witnesses because our goals spin out of alignment with God's. Our purposes are twisted to serve our own wants rather than our heavenly commission. This breeds apathy and envy. We shrink back from serving others and testifying to the gospel.

In fact, one of the chief problems in the church today is that we'll invite people to church, but not to Jesus. We have outsourced our evangelism. We are not called merely to lead people to a service, but to the Savior. This happens when you devalue your own testimony. When you neglect your own experience with the Lord, forget what he has done for you, or downplay his presence in your life, your thirst to evangelize is quenched. Because more than anything, we overcome the enemy in two ways. Listen to this mighty voice that John heard in heaven:

> Now the salvation and the power and the kingdom of our God and the authority of his Christ have come, for the accuser of our brothers has been thrown down, who accuses them day and night before our God. And they have conquered him by the blood of the Lamb and by the word of their testimony, for they loved not their lives even unto death. (Rev 12:10-11)

Our enemy is thrown down. The accuser is trampled and conquered by Jesus' blood and our testimonies. Can you believe that? Your testimony is part of God's great plan for redemption and defeating the powers of Hell. Have you made too little of what Jesus has done in your life? Have you neglected to wear these gospel shoes? If you have, the stakes are too high to do so any longer. Let the flames be rekindled in your heart and remember your first love. Wear these shoes and testify to Jesus. Truly, these are the most expensive shoes that were ever made. Because they were paid for by the very blood of God himself; the God who hung on the cross.

The Shield of Faith

Any time a believer is running in those shoes, the enemy is firing his hellish arrows. The flaming darts, however, are caught and extinguished by our shield of faith. Remember Satan's tactic of using doubt in our lives? That is an arrow meant to wound and divert us. But our faith becomes a shield—the deeper it grows, the stronger the shield.

Our faith is an overcoming faith, and cannot be quenched by any power on earth or in the spiritual realm. And this is not because of how strong we are, but because the object of our faith is God himself. Trusting in God is more of a sure thing than trusting in gravity to bring you back to the ground after you jump in the air. It's a safer bet than the sun rising in the morning and setting in the evening. Why? Because he flung stars from his fingertips into the inky black void of space. He set the planets spinning and breathed life into the dust that made mankind. If there is one person in whom to place our faith, it must be God and God alone. Who else can fulfill every promise? Who else has the power to speak and bend the world to his will?

Jesus spoke to the sea and made it calm. He took a step on water and it held solid beneath his feet. He gave thanks for a morsel of bread and fish and fed the multitudes. So what is it that you are up against in your life right now? What obstacle or trial are you facing? Is it as large as Mount Everest? Even if it is, it doesn't matter! Jesus said that if our faith was only as small as a mustard seed, we can still tell a mountain to move and it will obey (Matt 17:20). Our faith is strong because its object is strong—but weak when its object is weak.

When we take our eyes off of the Lord, we begin to lose faith. This is especially true during our trials. Paul wrote,

> So we do not lose heart. Though our outer self is wasting away, our inner self is being renewed day by day. For this light momentary affliction is preparing for us an eternal weight of glory beyond all comparison, as we look not to the things that are seen but to the things that are unseen. For the things that are seen are transient, but the things that are unseen are eternal. (2 Cor 4:16-18)

The shield of faith helps us to overcome any adversity because it looks not to the temporary, but to the eternal. Not to things that are passing away, but to things that the Lord has prepared for us. The things with a "weight of glory beyond all comparison." The shield of faith is a bedrock of our resolve. It is our stability, our confidence, and finds its strength in God.

The Helmet of Salvation

When we put down our shield of faith, we become increasingly vulnerable. But when we take off the helmet of salvation, we are truly defenseless. The enemy is strategic. So he most often aims for the two areas that have maximum impact on a human: the heart and the head. Our helmet of salvation is in place to keep our identity secure.

What state are we more at risk in than when we doubt our salvation? If the enemy can convince us that God has abandoned us or that Jesus couldn't possibly love us, then our helmet has hit the ground. But when we understand that the author of our salvation is not ourselves, but God himself, we can rest assured. We take this helmet off when we doubt what the Lord has done for us, or when we fear that his heart has grown cold toward us.

If you ever find yourself in this place, however, remember where we see God's heart for us shine most brightly. Who did he send to save you and me? His one and only Son. Can you doubt God's love for you and desire for your salvation when you realize that he sent his Son for you? That he paid our ransom by the life of Jesus? This keeps my helmet on. Anyone who would sacrifice their child for you has shown beyond a shadow of a doubt he loves you.

The Sword of the Spirit

God's love is shown in Jesus—and so is his power. Which brings us finally to the sword of the Spirit. This is our offensive weapon. But, it's only effective in our lives if we wield it. What power does a sword have that's left hanging on the wall? It might be nice to look at, but does it make you battle ready?

We neglect the sword of the Spirit when we neglect God's word. When we don't know the word of the Lord, we can't do any damage. That's where the power is at. In fact, look no further than Satan's temptation of Jesus that we studied earlier. What did Satan use to entice Jesus? He used Scripture. Even the enemy knows it's powerful, so he twists and wields it. But when we are filled with the word of God and live it out, we harness its unstoppable power. After all, how did Jesus combat Satan's lies? By cutting through the enemy's distortion with the word of truth.

OUR RESOLVE

As we face the enemy, God has not left us empty-handed. We are guarded, equipped, and exhorted to fight the good fight. Through these supernatural weapons, we can live lives worthy of our calling and fulfill our destinies. We can truly cross the Jordan and be transformed.

Imagine what your life would be like if you wholly surrendered to the Lord. Who would you be if you utterly belonged to God? How would your life look different than it does today? The gap between where you are right now and who God is calling you to be is the path of transformation. It is the perilous journey of the cross. But its rewards are rich, and this Promised Land is the only place where peace abounds.

I want to invite you into this resolution. A resolution to consecrate your will to God's. A submission of our life to his call and purpose. The pattern of transformation begins here. Intentional transformation happens as we are obedient. But we must listen to his voice and respond to his call. We must pray with Jesus in Gethsemane, "Nevertheless, not my will, but your will be done."

Dedicate yourself to the Lord for the joy he has set before you. Let me affirm that your best days are ahead of you. Your willingness to live intentionally and allow transformation to happen will be one of the best things you have ever done in your life. Our eyes have never seen nor our minds imagined what he has in store for us. Delight in the Lord, and he will give you the desires of your heart (Ps 37:4). He will transform you and make you new. He will lead you to the place of transformation. I am totally excited about the new you! If you missed it before, don't miss it again.

REFLECTION

1. Which spiritual weapon or piece of armor do you most often put down?
2. How can you pick it back up and use it in your spiritual warfare?
3. Which do you use most successfully? How can you teach someone else to use it?

7
THE PLACE

Transformation has both a pattern and a place. Just as Jesus has prepared a place for us, we can prepare a place to meet with him.

Toward the end of Jesus' earthly ministry, his disciples grew increasingly troubled. He predicted two betrayals: *one by Judas and one by Peter.* Judas would give·him up; Peter would deny him. Jesus knew exactly what was going to happen and how it would unfold. He also knew that the tomb wasn't his final destination, but rather a temporary place before his resurrection and ascension.

At the beginning of John 14, we see Jesus preparing his disciples for what is ahead, saying, "Let not your hearts be troubled. Believe in God; believe also in me. In my Father's house are many rooms. If it were not so, would I have told you that I go to prepare a place for you? And if I go and prepare a place for you, I will come again and will take you to myself, that where I am you may be also. And you know the way to where I am going." (John 14: 2-4)

Transformation happens in a place. And not just any place, but one that is specially made. One that is intentional, spiritual, and powerful. Jesus was preparing his disciples for his departure and leaving them with a new vision. This vision was of a new Comforter who would come, the Holy Spirit sent by the Father. Shortly after Jesus' death, resurrection, and ascension, we see this new vision fulfilled in tongues of fire! On this day, they were all together "in one place" when the Spirit fell (Acts 2:1).

There is power in an intentional space, consecrated for the fulfillment of the Lord's vision. Jesus promised to prepare a place for the disciples, and he also promised that the Spirit would come and bring transforming power. But he told them to wait together and pray until he arrived. You see, when we walk the path of intentional transformation we have studied in this book, we will always begin with obedience. Not obedience to a formula, a gimmick, or an equation. Not obedience to the words of man. But obedience to Jesus himself. Because he is the way, the truth, and the life. Godly transformation is only found in and through him.

When we are serious, we will be obedient to seek the Lord in a consecrated place, surrounded by people doing the same. The Lord honors and blesses that. When we make accommodations for a new vision as the disciples did, the Holy Spirit falls in power. Not because we followed a magic formula, but because we were obedient. The disciples' hearts were set on his Kingdom's advance from Jerusalem, to Judea, to Samaria, to the ends of the earth.

They were serious about God and his mission.

OBEDIENCE

Obedience. Let's take a minute and talk about this word. Since part of this book explores my transformation, I would be remiss if I didn't talk about what obedience means to me; and I believe I follow the mind of Christ here. Before you can obey something, you have to understand what it means to obey. In both the Hebrew and Greek language, the word primarily means the same thing. It means to *listen* to and to *hear* in both a *personal* and *relational* context. Looking through the eyes of the Old Testament, obedience follows the law-based interpretation:

1. Rule keeping;
2. Commandment compliance;
3. Performance according to precepts;
4. And works.

For me, because of the indwelling presence of the Holy Spirit and having a personal love-based faith and relationship, the laws of God are written on my heart (Heb 8:10). Jesus' obedience was not legalistic compliance to the law. His obedience was lived out by faith. His obedience was out of a love for the Kingdom and for his Father. He did not need an external system to mandate his obedience. He heard, he loved, and his will was already submitted in obedience.

I would like to say he simply followed what he was commissioned to do. When you love obedience, it is neither struggle, trial, nor test. Your willful commitment to love releases obedience. Jesus willingly followed his Father's voice and his plan. It's only when you have no agenda, no motive, and no plan of your own that you can understand this truth. It's easy to say yes when there is nothing else to answer to, when there is no other voice to listen to, and when there is no other plan to consider or look at.

Obedience is simply about fellowship. "And he said to all, 'If anyone would come after me, let him deny himself and take up his cross daily and *follow* me." (Luke 9:23, emphasis mine) Obedience is only a struggle when there is something else on the table. To paraphrase Proverbs 13:15, "it's the way of a transgressor that's hard." A transgressor struggles because they have a divided mind. A transgressor is one who violates or breaks a law, who offends it or goes beyond its limit. Again, it's not hard to obey when you are sold out to one thing. We see this in the book of Hebrews: "Then said I, Lo, I come to do thy will, O God." (10:7, KJV)

He didn't come to build his own kingdom. He didn't come to win a popularity contest. He came to follow the plan. He was sent to do what was already decided. When you are coerced, forced, or made to obey, that's not love. After all, Jesus said, "If you love me, you will keep my commandments." (John 14:15) This is how I serve and worship. I am free to obey, and free to disobey. I am free to love with all of my heart, and I am free not to love with all my heart. I am neither a slave nor a prisoner. I choose to love. When I love,

I obey. For me, these two words cannot be separated. My obedience is the fruit and proof of my love, and my love is the fruit and proof of my obedience. I quote from the *Now Testament* out of the book of Judy chapter 1, verse 1: "Lo, I come in the volume of this book it is already written of me to do thy will." And there is no other truth for me! This is my *resolve*!

THE PLACE OF TRANSFORMATION

You can follow the disciples' lead and create an intentional place as well. In fact, not only *can* you, but you *must*. Transformation has both a pattern and a place. And this place is more than a destination, it is also the path along the way. The upper room was the place where transformation happened—but transformation also happened on the way there.

To prepare this place requires a sole focus on Jesus himself. It means that we cut the clutter. If something doesn't catalyze your momentum, movement, and progress toward godly transformation, it has to go. Here's the test for anything: *Does it increase your love and hunger for Jesus?* If it doesn't, it's gone. Resolve to cling to nothing but Jesus. Just like Jacob, who wrestled with God through the night, create a place in your home that is wholly dedicated to your pursuit of God. It could be in your basement, in a closet, or an office. It doesn't matter. What does matter is that it's dedicated to meeting with God.

The Right Environment

We have spent much time discerning the patterns of the Kingdom and of the enemy. I have shared how I have seen both in my life. So, as we draw to a finish, I would like to share with you how I have made this space in my life. When I think about my meeting space with the Lord, one word comes to mind: sanctuary. It is a refuge, tucked away from the bustle and distractions of life. It is a focused environment; a serene place where I find rest. And I always have it ready.

There is always a journal, a pencil, and music ready for action. It's a place where I am always prepared to hear from the Lord—and where I expect to! It is a place where my spiritual formation occurs. Where I reaffirm my whole-hearted commitment to the Lord, and the stage is always set for the play to begin. But most importantly, I keep this space as an act of obedience, worship, and urgency. I believe that Jesus has gone to prepare a place for me, and this is the place I have prepared for him.

My goal and desire is always to encounter Christ. I want what is old in me to pass away so that all things can become new. And this is a place of renewing, of refreshing, and of vision. If you are serious about transformation, then create a space for it to happen. Dedicate an area to meet with the Lord—and when you do, don't be surprised when you find him waiting to greet you. To be obedient followers of Jesus and powerful warriors in the Kingdom, we must hear his voice and act on it. So as you seek him in this consecrated place, do so with feet that are ready to run with the gospel and a spirit that is ready to go to war. Meet with the Lord and be transformed.

REFLECTION

1. Do you have a place dedicated only to seeking the Lord?
2. How would it be an act of obedience to create one?
3. What transformation do you believe the Lord is leading you to?

CONCLUSION

My desire is that this book has inspired you to act—and act intentionally so that your life is changed. But you can't be forced, pressured, or made to obey. If it's not willful, intentional, and strictly out of love for God, it means there remains something in your life you've placed a higher value upon. My prayer is you will now take what the Lord has revealed to you and put it to use.

Obedience is the first step on any journey with Jesus. Have you intentionally made a place to meet with him? Have you set aside room in your life to feast on the word and gain greater revelation of our God? Will you obey the call to arms in prayer and take up the weapons and armor he's provisioned us with?

I hope you will. Because if you do, you will experience a new reality, a new vision, and unexpected transformation. As you pursue this, remember my friend Jerome, the friend the Lord used to help me see what I could not. Remember the vision that unlocked my future and unpacked my life.

Remember Mordecai, who showed Esther that she was made for "such a time as this," causing her vision and destiny to expand and unfold. Remember the teacher at Fort Thompson, who followed his friend's footsteps and responded to God's call, leaving that service a totally different man. The greater vision and truth is that we are not being transformed for our own sake alone—but we are transformed in community.

We are one body made of many parts. And as you grow, so do I. That's how it works. Our obedience is multiplied for the benefit of our brothers and sisters. So, as you walk this journey, I invite you to connect with me. I want to hear your testimony; I want to hear your story of transformation! I want to learn about the place you have set aside and how God has met you there. I want to see how the Holy Spirit is working in you—because as he works in you, he works in me, too. And together, we will encourage people across our global network to seek intentional transformation.

"You are a child of God. Your playing small does not serve the world."

Marianne Williams

ABOUT THE AUTHOR

Judy, born in Kingsville, Texas, is a pioneer, spiritual leader and a sought-after global speaker who has commanded the attention of many audiences.

Reared in Buffalo, New York, Judy was mentored and trained in ministry by her father, Bishop C. Roberson (COGIC). It was during those years, she assisted her father in establishing churches in the western New York region as well as serving administratively at the local church. In 1984, at the age of 32, Judy received a National appointment from the COGIC under the General Supervisor Mother M. McGlothen as the Jurisdictional Supervisor of Eastern South Dakota Women's Auxiliary. Judy was celebrated as the Youngest Supervisor ever given that appointment in the history of COGIC organization.

Characterized by her friends and colleagues as one of the most insightful, powerful and compassionate women today, Judy boldly confronts individuals to know their life's purpose and ministry. She warms the heart, stirs the human spirit, and challenges her audiences to connect with their life's purpose. She's been known to shift cultures and change nations.

Judy has traveled to more than 25 plus foreign countries and has spoken before presidents of nations, to groups as small as 10 and to audiences as large as 35,000, releasing prophetic insight into those regions. Also, she's the Sr. Leader of Center of Life Church, a multi-ethnic fellowship in the heart of Sioux Falls, South Dakota. Judy oversees churches and ministries in and outside of her region. For 20+ years Judy is yet on staff at Keystone Chemical Detox Center in Canton, SD where she is one of the leading Spiritual Counselors.

In 1986, Judy started the Center of Life Church in Sioux Falls, South Dakota. By 2003, three other churches were birthed. Deeper Life (Indian Reservation), New Life Church (Sioux City, Iowa) and New Life Russian Church of Sioux Falls, South Dakota.

Judy serves as a personal advisor to many in the business and entertainment industries. She is involved in a number of successful businesses, where she lends strategic and spiritual insight towards reaching their full potential.

Judy is a graduate of Bryant and Stratton College, Buffalo, NY, studied at Houghton Bible College, School of Management at State University in New York, and worked as a licensed realtor for fifteen years.

Being a thirty two year resident of Sioux Falls, she is actively involved in the community, where she has served two terms on the City's **Human Relations** Commission, three years on the County Commissioner's Diversity Board, as well as holding a position in human relations as a liaison person for the City.

She is the president of the Judy Shaw Foundation, a Philan-thropic non-profit org. Building schools, orphanages and building lives.

Contact Judy at ajshaw53@gmail.com

INTENTIONAL TRANSFORMATION

By Judy Shaw

Intentional Transformation is a practical text, an easy read, that will provide you, the reader with a spiritually moving experience. My text will challenge you to delve into the depths of your inner most being, ask yourself critical questions, renounce every excuse, every hindrance and justifiable action, all for the purpose of getting the rest of God's Best for your life. It is for those who are willing to seek the undiscovered you. My friend, Simon Bailey, author of the best seller, Release Your Brilliance, challenges us to find our brilliance that we were born with. Intentional Transformation screams, find it and then the scream gets louder, find it now! **Intentional Transformation** demands that you be the self-acting agent in this process and that you give no resistance to the work of the Holy Spirit who will participate and partner with you to finish this work. **Intentional Transformation** is so powerful. It doesn't wait until the end to yield change, it starts as soon as you start.

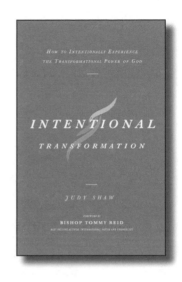

— Judy Shaw

ISBN: 978-1-945255-16-8 • Copyright © Judy Shaw Foundation

ORDER FORM

You may order by credit card at mariahpress.com. mariahpresssales@midconetwork.com
Mariah Press: 605-367-6913

Name: _____

Address:_____

City:_____ State: _____ Zip:_____

Phone: _____ E-mail: _____

Cost per book: $14.95; plus tax; plus postage
___ Copies; Order Amount: _____
Minimum postage: $10. Postage will be determined by order size.

Make Payment to:
Mariah Press
2420 S. Center Avenue
Sioux Falls, South Dakota 57105